Skate Parks
ON A ROLL!

By Chip Lovitt

CELEBRATION PRESS

Pearson Learning Group

Contents

One Town's Skate Park Story

Skateboarders in Bethel, Connecticut, are lucky. When they want to grind a rail or roll down a **quarterpipe**, they just head toward school! Next to Bethel's Johnson Elementary School is a 16,000-square-foot skate park. When school's out and the weather's warm, you're likely to find a crowd of young skaters launching themselves off any of the 11 obstacles in the park.

Bethel's skateboarders make stunts like the **ollie**— a no-hands aerial move—look easy. Getting Bethel's skate park built, however, was anything but easy.

A skater at Bethel Skate Park

Bethel is a small Connecticut town 60 miles northeast of New York City. Both kids and parents had to work hard to get their skate park built. They also had to work just as hard to keep it open.

Before they had a skate park, Bethel's skaters were sometimes viewed as a nuisance. Some local merchants didn't like having skaters cruising by their stores.

In early 1999, Peter Wise, the father of a Bethel skateboarder, had an idea. "I kept seeing more and more articles in the local paper saying that the town needed to do something about the kids skating downtown," he says. "There was a need for a safe place where kids could skate." Bethel had baseball, football, and soccer fields. *Why not build a skate park?* Wise wondered.

He took the idea to the town's governing board and got positive feedback. He and other parents formed a committee to study the idea. They made speeches and gave presentations to several other town agencies, including the Planning and Zoning Commission and the Park and Recreation Department. Feedback was positive, and the local police liked the idea, too. There was a problem, however: finding a site. There was a shortage of open, available land in Bethel.

After many meetings, the town gave its approval to

Some of the equipment at Bethel Skate Park

put the park next to Johnson School. Skaters were involved with the skate park committee from the start. They attended town meetings and helped raise money for the ramps. They had a big say in the design and equipment for the park.

The Bethel Skate Park opened in 2000. A huge success, it drew more than 60 kids its first weekend. The skaters didn't know it then, but there were still a few snags ahead for the park.

Bethel is not unique. Many towns across the country have built public skate parks. According to industry figures, there may be as many as 1,000 skate parks in the United States today.

A Short History of Skateboarding

Kids have been riding boards with wheels since the early 1900s. A century ago, kids would nail a wooden milk crate to a wooden plank and add roller-skate wheels. Commercially produced skateboards didn't roll onto the scene until the late 1950s. Early boards had clay wheels. They gave skateboarders more control than metal wheels did.

In the 1960s, the surfing craze hit America like a tidal wave. Ocean surfers used surfboards. Street surfers made all kinds of homemade skateboards. The new craze was called sidewalk surfing, and California was its center. Skateboarding contests took place. Surfboard companies began mass-producing skateboards. From 1962 to 1965, more than 50 million skateboards were sold.

The fad crashed to a halt by the middle of the 1960s. Early skateboards were hard to control. The clay wheels that were being attached to boards didn't provide enough **traction** for skaters. Some skaters were injured, and many towns banned the sport. Orders for new skateboards were canceled. The sport didn't go away completely, but it looked as if its popularity had faded.

Early skateboards were difficult for riders to control.

In the early 1970s, changes were made to make skateboards safer. New wheels were made from **urethane**, a plasticlike substance. These new wheels had more gripping power. Wider boards made skateboards more stable. Smoothly spinning ball-bearing wheels came out in 1975.

Thanks to these improvements, skateboarding made a comeback. In 1976, the first skate park was built in Florida. By 1979, there were about 300 skate parks in the United States. Most of them were in California.

A skater executes
an ollie.

   In the late 1970s,
something happened
that would change
skateboarding forever.
A skater named Alan
Gelfand created a new
move called an ollie. While
rolling along, Gelfand would launch
himself and his board into the air in a no-hands aerial
move. Soon, skateboarders were going "vertical,"
skating up and down on ramps and doing tricks on
any sloping surfaces they could find. A new style of
stunt-based "street skating" took off—but so did
insurance costs. By 1980, skate parks were shutting
down once again due to **liability** issues. Park owners
and town recreation departments could not afford to
insure themselves against possible lawsuits brought
by injured riders.

The sport, however, refused to die. Skaters built homemade ramps and took to the streets. They used curbs and concrete steps to come up with all kinds of daring moves. This aggressive style of skating brought new energy to the sport. Before long, professional skateboarding competitions offering prize money were being held. In the 1980s, pro skaters such as Tony Hawk entered the spotlight.

Street skating wasn't popular with everyone. Many towns viewed skaters as a problem. Some banned street skating. In the early 1990s, however, skateboarding got a boost when in-line skating became popular. Once again, skate parks began to pop up across the country.

People noticed that the parks got many skaters off the street. Parks also gave skaters a safer place to skate. Public ideas about skaters slowly began to change. Many towns came to see skateboarding as a sport that deserved support and its own space.

Skateboarding by the Numbers

According to industry estimates, there are:
- 16 million skateboarders in the United States.
- 300+ companies producing skateboards and skateboard accessories, generating more than $1 billion in annual sales.
- 700–1,000 public skate parks in the United States.
- 3 new skate parks opening each week.

Getting a Park Rolling

American skate parks come in all shapes and sizes. Small-town skate parks can range from 3,000 to 5,000 square feet. At the other end of the scale is Denver, Colorado's 50,000-square-foot skate park.

Skate parks get started in many ways. In some towns, the park and recreation department is a driving force. Hornell, New York's skate park was sponsored by the local Kiwanis Club, a service organization. In Greenwood, Indiana, a local skate shop provided money and support. In most cases, however, kids and parents work together to make a park happen.

Denver's skate park is the largest free public skate facility in the United States.

©Walk Upshaw

Chatham Township, New Jersey, is a good example of this. Located 25 miles west of New York City, Chatham Township has about 10,000 residents. Its skate park has been three years in the making. The town will spend over $240,000 to build a 10,800-square-foot skate park.

In 1999, Chatham residents Suzanne Bonamo and Mary Carnes both had teenage sons who skateboarded. "They skated first in driveways," Carnes recalls. "As their skills grew, they skated around school, in the post office plaza, any places where there were steps or sidewalks with curbing." It was Bonamo's son who first raised the question: Why couldn't Chatham build a skate park?

Bonamo and Carnes talked it over and agreed that Chatham needed a safe place where kids could skateboard and do in-line skating. "There was not a skate park within a 25-mile radius," Carnes says.

A sports survey had recently been done in Chatham's schools. Nearly 300 kids said they either skateboarded or did in-line skating. "We used this number to show the town that a skate park was needed," Carnes explains. "We made speeches to the Board of Education, the Board of Recreation, and many other groups." The response was a flood of questions. What about liability, insurance, and safety? Where would the park be located? What would it look like?

The committee did a great deal of research, much of it online. They contacted people all across the country. The idea gained momentum as other kids and parents joined the effort.

Chatham's committee set out to raise public awareness about the skate park. They printed a brochure and bumper stickers and put together a video. "We videotaped kids as they skated and parks we visited to show what a skate park looked like," Carnes says. "We talked to whomever would listen to us—the Kiwanis Club, League of Women Voters, local businesses, realtors, civic groups—and asked for donations."

Bumper stickers and brochures helped raise public awareness about the Chatham Skate Park.

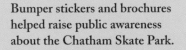

In late 2000, the town approved the skate park, but only if the committee could raise the money to build it and if the right site could be found. "We finally settled on an undeveloped piece of property—a field next to the police station," Carnes explains. "Once the town donated the site, we announced that we were holding organizational meetings."

A budget was drawn up. "We were hoping to do the park for $100,000–$150,000, but there's always something unexpected," Carnes points out. "Once we started, we found railroad ties and vegetative material that had to be removed from the site." That cost pushed the park's price tag up to well over $200,000. The Chatham Township government committed up to $100,000 to prepare the site. The residents would raise the rest of the funds.

The committee organized fact-finding trips to skate parks in neighboring states. The kids skated in the parks to decide what equipment they liked and the flow and layout they preferred. The skaters also spoke out at town meetings and had a lot of input into the design.

"We assigned them in pairs to sketch out the park themselves," Carnes says. "They made 3-D cardboard cutouts of different skate elements." Using those ideas, the committee contacted skate park builders, asking for cost estimates. Chatham's park will open in 2003.

Algonac, Michigan, is a city of about 4,600 located 40 miles northeast of Detroit. Its 7,200-square-foot skate park opened in the summer of 2002. Like the parks in Bethel and Chatham, Algonac's grew out of a need for a safe place for young people to skate. "Algonac has no sidewalks for the most part, and kids were skating in the streets," says Cindy Babisz of Algonac's Downriver Recreation Commission (DRC).

"The city was tired of chasing skaters from storefront and park areas," adds Algonac's Brad Durasa. A skate park supporter, Durasa is the father of two teenaged in-line skaters. A downtown improvement project was already set to begin in Algonac, and the city had hired a planning firm to give a report on the project. The report said that a skate park should be included in the plan.

In November 2000, the city and the DRC called a meeting of skaters and parents to discuss building a skate park. There was a big turnout, and the city council was encouraged enough to proceed.

The DRC, skaters, and their parents quickly launched a campaign to sell the idea. "We did a survey," Durasa says. "We collected page after page of supportive comments from local citizens and presented them to the Algonac City Council. They further convinced the city government there was strong support for a skate park."

A month later, a committee of skaters, parents, and officials was formed. Their goal was to come up with a design and budget. Using the Internet, the skaters looked at other skate parks, trying to decide what kind of equipment they wanted.

The city gave the go-ahead to put the site in a field next to a school. The park would be in downtown Algonac, in a site surrounded by busy streets and near the police station. The park had to be visible to residents and police. Durasa explains, "We wanted as many eyes on it as we could get."

By April 2001, the committee had a plan. In May, one of the skaters presented it to a public meeting of the city council. The other young people at the meeting cheered when the council voted to approve funding for the park.

The city would supply the land and pay for fencing and paving the concrete pad. The skaters would have to come up with a whopping $50,000 for the ramps. Could they do it? It would take a year of hard work— and an unexpected stroke of luck—to make it happen.

Skater Dustin Durasa presented the Algonac Skate Park Committee's plan to the city council.

Finding the Funds

A town can approve a plan for a skate park, but that doesn't mean the park always gets built. Building a skate park not only takes hard work and persistence; it also takes money—lots of it.

In the case of Bethel's skate park, skaters were quick to pitch in. "We held car washes," Peter Wise recalls, "lots of them. They raised more than $1,200." Wise also asked for contributions from the various town businesses. "I knocked on every door in town," he says. Sometimes donations came in the form of services. The Bethel Jaycees donated half the costs of a shed. A logging company cleared the site for free. A construction company bulldozed it. The company Mr. Wise works for, Ouidad Hair Products, donated $15,000 to pay for the ramps.

Algonac's skaters were also involved right from the start. "During our summer carnival," Brad Durasa says, "kids carried signs that said 'Let's Build a Skate Park!' and collected donations in a plastic jug. A car wash raised $1,000 in one afternoon. A local skater drew a design for our fundraiser T-shirts, and we made over $1,000 selling them. We sold flower bulbs and cookie dough. In six months, we raised $10,000."

The Algonac Skate Park committee was still $40,000 short of its goal. "The kids never gave up," Durasa recalls. "We knew if we kept picking away, something good would happen."

Something good did happen. Earlier in the year, Brad's son, Dustin, had applied for a grant from the Tony Hawk Foundation.

Hawk is widely considered to be the best skateboarder in the world. He is the only skateboarder ever to do a "900," a midair twist with two and one-half full rotations. Before retiring in 1999, he had won every major skateboarding contest. Hawk also invented more than 50 skateboarding tricks.

The goal of Hawk's non-profit foundation is to

promote and help finance public skate parks. The foundation favors parks that keep local skaters involved in the design process. The group gives out awards ranging from $5,000 to $25,000 to qualified skate park projects. The foundation was so impressed by Algonac's fundraising efforts that it gave the city a grant of $10,000. That helped the city manager apply for and obtain matching funds. The county and the local youth advisory council each gave $10,000.

Chatham's skaters and parents started their fundraising by setting up tables at local family events and asking for contributions. They sold T-shirts through the local sports shop. Skaters who played in bands did benefit concerts to raise money and support for the park. A high-school group worked with a middle-school group to collect used sports equipment for a rummage sale. At the local parochial school, a service club held bake sales that raised $400.

Chatham's skate park committee asked local businesses and civic groups for donations. Private citizens also pitched in. An anonymous donor agreed to give $5,000 if the committee could raise an equal amount. It did. A local foundation gave $15,000. Adult fundraising events made another $30,000. Chatham was well on the way to meeting its goal.

How Skate Parks Are Designed

If you look carefully as you drive along Interstate 95 through the city of Bridgeport, Connecticut, you'll see an odd sight. There, in a factory parking lot, is a large, state-of-the-art **halfpipe**. The factory is the home of Rampage, a company that builds skate parks. The U-shaped curving ramp shows people what the factory builds. The halfpipe can also be used by anyone who wants to check out Rampage's work.

Visitors to the factory hear the shrieking sounds of metal being cut, drilled, welded, and hammered into shape. Metal frames that will soon become skateboard

a halfpipe

ramps sit stacked in front of the building. Rampage has built more than 100 skate parks since 1992, including Bethel's.

Richard Peterson is an owner of Rampage. A contractor and carpenter by profession, Peterson got into the skate park business almost by accident.

"My two sons were skateboarders in Trumbull, Connecticut," he says. "We started lobbying the town to have a skate park built. After two and one-half years, we finally got it approved. We went on the Internet and did a search for companies that made skate parks and ramps. There were plenty of companies out there, but none of them had a product we thought would last long enough to give the town its money's worth. So we started designing our own ramps."

Peterson ended up building Trumbull's park, using both steel-framed ramps and concrete ones. Since then, Rampage has built ramps at skate parks from Maine to California and as far away as Alaska and Cuba.

Once a town is ready to build a park, Peterson says, "there are usually two ways it goes. The local skaters may come up with a design. The town puts it into a bid form that they send out to different ramp companies. The other way is to have the park professionally designed."

Kids should be involved in the design process,

Peterson says. "It gives them a sense of ownership in their own park. We take their ideas, and we start laying the equipment out."

Rampage's designers make a model by laying out half-inch scale ramps on a metal board. "We take a digital picture of it and e-mail the layout to the town," Peterson explains. "They review it and e-mail it back to us." At the same time, the company figures out what the different pieces of the design will cost. These figures are sent to the skate park committee and the town.

Different types of material can be used to build skate park equipment. Concrete, steel, and wood are three basic materials. Wood-based ramps tend to be less expensive.

Concrete is a popular building material for skate parks.

However, wood does not last as long as concrete or steel. In place of wood, Rampage sometimes uses a steel frame covered with a type of **laminate** board. This board is sold under different brand names, including Skatelite®.

Concrete parks are also popular, especially in warmer climates. Concrete ramps are subject to cracking. This problem is bigger in areas with cold winters. Because of this, concrete parks need to be inspected regularly for cracks or surface damage.

Parks built with concrete are more expensive than those built with wood or steel. A poured-in-place concrete park could cost hundreds of thousands of dollars. In contrast, an average free-standing park made of steel or wood-framed ramps would cost about $60,000–$70,000. There are also **hybrid** parks—ones that combine free-standing ramps with concrete features such as bowls.

In planning a park, a town takes into account how many skaters are likely to use it. If a town has only 3,000 people, a small skate park or skate plaza might serve the skaters very well.

There's more to designing a skate park than choosing ramps. Traffic patterns and safety have to be addressed. "The flow of the park is very important," Peterson explains, "especially when there are both in-line skaters and skateboarders using the park. They need to keep up their speed when they go from one obstacle to the next. It's nice to have many different traffic patterns, but you also have to minimize crossing patterns. Pedestrian safety around the **perimeter** is also very important because of flying boards and flying kids." A fence that is 3 or 4 feet high can help to protect people passing by.

Ramp safety is also a concern. "Ramps over 3 or 4 feet tall should have safety railings around the deck areas," Peterson points out. Ramps also should be made in such a way that there's nothing the skater could run into. Ramps should not have any sharp edges, points, or high screws.

In addition to thinking about materials, skate park builders work with a town to plan the features the park will have. Certain features, such as quarterpipes, **grind rails**, **bank ramps**, and **launch ramps**, are standard. However, Peterson says, there should always be unique elements to every park.

The design for Algonac's skate park called for ten features, including nine wood-framed ramps with Skatelite® surfaces. Algonac chose to use wood both for budget and for design reasons. The committee wanted to be able to move or alter the ramps at a later date, if they chose to. A concrete park does not offer this choice.

Algonac's skaters can kick off their ride by launching

The layout for the Algonac Skate Park

Equipment Key

A. Start Box
B. Quarterpipe
C. Quarterpipe
D. Sidecar
E. Grind Rail
F. Fun Box Half Pyramid
G. Launch Box
H. Quarterpipe
I. Wedge
J. Mini Ramp

themselves off a 7-foot-high start box with a rail. The start box has a 12-foot-wide ramp with a flat platform as a starting point and a low metal rail. Skaters can jump on the rail and slide down it, or "grind." Nearby are two quarterpipes, one 5 feet tall and another narrower one that is 3 feet tall. These curved ramps look like one side of a halfpipe.

Skaters can do a variety of aerial moves and jumps off the sidecar at Algonac. Its low ramps lead up to a flat tabletop. It also has a grind rail and another flat tabletop to jump off. Near the sidecar sits a free-standing grind rail. Skaters get airborne, then slide down the rail with their boards.

A pro skater does a board slide down a rail.

A fun box has a ramp leading up to a tabletop and a ramp down. Algonac has its own variation: a fun box and half pyramid. The half pyramid's ramps rise from 2 to 6 feet. The ramps surround the flat top. This structure is joined on one side by a launch box. Skaters can ride up the launch ramp, do an ollie on the wide, flat top, then ride down a second flat ramp.

Algonac's skate park, like many others, also serves in-line skaters. They skate up and down the ramps and do their own tricks, jumps, and aerial moves.

Other features, such as bowls and high railings, can also be added to a skate park. The only limits to a park's design are the space available and the funding. The possibilities are endless.

Keeping It Rolling

Keeping a skate park rolling after it opens takes a lot of work. Bethel's park opened for its second season in spring 2001. The original skate park committee, whose purpose had been to build the park, made plans to disband at the end of the year.

For a while, a local skateboard shop helped to maintain and supervise the park. The shop rented helmets and sold equipment but couldn't make enough of a profit to keep running the park. In early 2002, the original committee asked the town and the local Parks and Recreation Department to take over the park.

That plan soon ran into a roadblock. Bethel was having budget problems. The town had no money to staff the park. During winter 2002, it looked as if the park might not open again.

Luckily, a group of parents and their kids stepped up to the task. They formed a new committee and offered to run the park as an all-volunteer effort. Parents ran local soccer, football, and baseball leagues in much the same way.

"We suggested that the kids run the park with adult supervision," says Nancy LoBalbo, a committee member. The town agreed, and the park was saved.

Bethel skaters above the age of 14 serve as monitors, collect the $3.00 daily fee, and sell water. They also enforce safety rules, making sure skaters wear helmets and follow the park rules. They ask all skaters and parents to sign a **waiver**, or release form. The signers agree not to hold the park or town responsible for any injury. Some teen skaters also serve on the committee and attend town meetings.

Skate parks such as Bethel's usually post their rules. Here are some typical skate park rules.

Skate Park Safety Rules

1. Skaters must wear helmets.
2. Skaters must sign in and provide emergency contact in case of injury.
3. A liability waiver must be signed.
4. All skaters under the age of 11 must be accompanied by an appropriate guardian over the age of 16.
5. Pads and wristbands are strongly recommended (and often required).
6. Skaters should show the good behavior expected for participation sports, including good sportsmanship. No fighting, teasing, or bullying is allowed.
7. No glass containers, drugs, alcohol, or tobacco products are allowed in the park.
8. No graffiti is permitted.
9. All trash must be disposed of properly.

Fundraising doesn't stop once a skate park opens. Bethel's skate park committee is still raising money to finish paying for its fence. They also hope to purchase more ramps for their park. "It really is a work in progress," says Nancy LoBalbo.

Once a park is built, towns often plan new features to make it even better. Algonac's skaters hope to raise more funds so they can add some bleachers for spectators. They'd also like to put together a "loan closet" of helmets and pads that parents and kids will be able to sign out. In Lakewood, Washington, local skaters want to install outdoor lighting for their skate park. They worked with the Lions Club to start a fundraising drive to raise $15,000 for the lights.

Parks can also need repairs. "Ramps do require some maintenance over time," says Rampage's Richard Peterson. "We make follow-up visits and check for surface damage. We look at the fasteners that hold railings and look for wear on the grind edges. We make sure all nuts and bolts are secure and that none of them have been tampered with or are missing." Wooden ramps need more maintenance. Many use very small screws that can pop out or break off. The ramps need to be inspected and fixed for the safety of the skaters.

Skaters who help to get a skate park built in their town learn some important lessons. Nancy LoBalbo

Skaters who help build their
town skate park learn about
local government.

says of Bethel's
skaters, "They've
learned to
negotiate the
system. They've
learned about the
town government and
how it works. If you want
something, you have to put
something into it. Nobody gets anything for free."
Algonac's skaters have also benefited in other ways
from their new park. "The kids have had a positive
and realistic experience with the city," Brad Durasa
says. "They asked the city for something, worked out
the details, and then kept their side of the bargain.
These kids don't feel like outsiders anymore."

Algonac's skaters took their involvement with the city a step further in August 2002. They went before the Algonac City Council and proposed a new law that would ban trick skating in business parking lots and public parks. "By stepping forward with a solution to the problem, the skaters will gain the respect of the council and the community," Durasa says. "This way, the skaters will have a say in how the law reads. We do not want the law written in a way that would hassle kids going to and from the skate park."

The future looks exciting for skaters and skate parks. "Skating is not a passing phase like hula hoops," says Bethel's Peter Wise. "It's a new generation of sport."

"With national competitions such as the Gravity Games and the X Games, and more and more parks being built all over the country, skating has become mainstream," says Richard Peterson. "Snowboarding became an Olympic sport recently, and it will not be long before board sports and in-line skating sports are in the Olympics. This is not just a fad."

Will one of these skate parks produce a future Olympian? Nobody knows, but one thing is sure. Skate parks are here to stay!

 Glossary

bank ramp   a tall, steep, flat-surfaced, triangle-shaped ramp

grind rail   a thin metal rail used by a skater to slide the board sideways in a grinding motion

halfpipe   a steep, curving, U-shaped ramp with an open, flat area at its bottom

hybrid   a combination of varied elements blended together

laminate   made from compressed layers of a substance, such as wood, paper, or fabric

launch ramp   a short, low ramp often used to get up onto other pieces of equipment

liability   an insurance term; the state of being liable, or responsible, for the negative results of an action, such as an injury or equipment damage

ollie   a midair move performed without hands

perimeter   outer edge or boundary

quarterpipe   a half of a halfpipe; a steep, curving ramp with a flat, open bottom

traction   the power of an object or objects to grip or hold a surface while moving, without slipping

urethane   a plasticlike substance

waiver   a release form